Service Dogs

by Jessica Rudolph

Consultant: Karen Shirk
Executive Director, 4 Paws For Ability, Inc.
Xenia, Ohio

BEARPORT
PUBLISHING

New York, New York

Credits

Cover and Title Page, © Huntstock/Thinkstock; 4, © iStockphoto/Thinkstock;
4–5, © John Walker/Fresno Bee/MCT; 6–7, © National Geographic Image Collection/
Alamy; 8–9, © Mark M. Murray/The Republican/Landov; 10–11, © ARCO/J De
Meester; 12–13, © Libby Welch/Alamy; 14–15, © REX USA/Jonathan Banks;
16, © Julian Pottage/Alamy; 16–17, © Jacqulyn Maisonneuve/Sipa Press/;
18, © Disability Images/Alamy; 18–19, © Julian Pottage/Alamy; 20–21, © Associated
press; 22, © Chuck Wagner/Shutterstock; 23TL, © Steve Lyne; 23TR, © Mark M.
Murray/The Republican/Landov; 23BL, © Libby Welch/Alamy; 23BR, © Arterra
Picture Library/Alamy.

Publisher: Kenn Goin
Creative Director: Spencer Brinker
Design: Debrah Kaiser
Photo Researcher: Picture Perfect Professionals, LLC

Library of Congress Cataloging-in-Publication Data

Rudolph, Jessica.
  Service dogs / by Jessica Rudolph.
     pages cm — (Bow-WOW! dog helpers)
  Includes bibliographical references and index.
  Audience: Age 5–8
  ISBN 978-1-62724-121-2 (library binding) — ISBN 1-62724-121-3 (library binding)
  1. Service dogs—Juvenile literature. I. Title.
  HV1569.6.R83 2014
  362.4'048—dc23
                              2013036953

For more information, write to Bearport Publishing Company, Inc., 45 West 21st Street, Suite 3B,
New York, New York 10010. Printed in the United States of America.

10 9 8 7 6 5 4 3 2 1

Contents

Meet a Service Dog

I'm a **service dog**.

My owner is deaf.

I let her know about sounds she can't hear.

Ruff! Ruff!

4

Service dog

Handler

A person who owns a service dog is called a handler.

Service dogs let handlers know when alarm clocks go off. How?

We nudge handlers with our paws.

A service dog can let its deaf handler know when the doorbell rings. The dog nudges the handler. Then it runs to the door.

Some service dogs help people with **disabilities.**

We stay by their sides all day.

We even go with them to work or school.

Some people with disabilities can't walk. Others can't see or hear.

Service dogs use their mouths to help people in wheelchairs.

We carry objects.

We pick up things that fall.

A service dog can use its nose to turn on lights.

Other service dogs help people who are ill.

Some people have seizures.

A seizure can make a person shake.

A person who has a seizure may pass out.

13

Service dogs
help people who
have seizures.

We press a special
button on the phone.

We call the hospital.

Service dogs may try
to wake their handlers
after a seizure. They
lick their owners' faces.

How do dogs learn
to help people?

As puppies, we go
to school.

We learn **commands**
such as "stay."

Any size dog can
be a service dog.

During training, service dogs learn different jobs.

We carry keys in our mouths.

We press elevator buttons with our paws.

Service dogs need to be calm. They learn not to jump on people.

IN CASE
OF
FIRE
DO NOT USE
ELEVATORS

USE
STAIRS

After training, service dogs live with their new owners.

We do amazing things for our handlers.

We are always happy to help!

Some service dogs know as many as 90 commands!

Service Dog Facts

- Service dogs may go places where other dogs are not allowed, such as grocery stores.

- Do not pet a service dog without asking its handler for permission. The dog is working and needs to pay attention to its owner.

- Many service dogs wear special jackets or capes. They let people know the dogs are working.

commands (kuh-MANDZ) orders given by people to do something

disabilities (*diss*-uh-BIL-uh-teez) conditions that make it hard for people to do everyday things

seizures (SEE-zhurz) sudden attacks that can cause a person to shake or even pass out

service dog (SUR-viss DAWG) a dog that is trained to do tasks for a person who has a disability or health problem

Index

Read More

Jusino, Cindy M. *My Service Dog: One Way a Boy Got Help With His Sensory Processing Disorder.* Oswego, IL: Sensational Publications (2013).

Winokur, Donnie Kanter. *Nuzzle: Love Between a Boy and His Service Dog.* Brooklyn Park, MN: Better Endings New Beginnings (2011).

Learn More Online

To learn more about service dogs, visit
www.bearportpublishing.com/Bow-WOW!

About the Author

Jessica Rudolph lives in Connecticut. She has edited and written many books about history, science, and nature for children.